Sam,

You have been a blessing to me.

Bart

LIFE'S LESSONS FOR THE HUNTER

BART MCMILLAN

GAINESVILLE, GEORGIA 30506

Life's Lessons For The Hunter

ACKNOWLEDGMENTS

This book is dedicated to my Mom and Dad, who allowed me to learn through life and hunting. Some of the greatest lessons I have learned have been at the expense of their worry and fear over my freedom to enjoy the sport of hunting. I truly want to thank my mother for being a mom who always asked, "Do you have enough on?" and my dad who was always there to help me clean the harvest when I was too tired. I must say a word of thanks to my hunting partners during the years; Dad, Eddie, Frank, Billy Joe, Kerry, Damon, Mr. Lively, Butch, Rip, Blake, Josh, Les, beloved Eddie, Poncho, John, Dr. Taylor, David, Tyler, Mr. Sinclair, Phillip, Danny, Brick, Mike, Sam, Michael, Charlie, Jay, Denny, my sons Micah and Matthew, daughter Macie, and my greatest partner, my wife Ocie, who always said, "Go." And a special thanks to my Savior Jesus Christ who was with me on every hunt.

In writing this book, I looked to some of my friends who I respect so much to help guide me. Thank you John, Mike, Cinda, and Petina.

A word from the author:
Life's Lessons For The Hunter

This book is written to for hunters about real hunts. I know you will enjoy this book because of the stories, but also because it will challenge you to look at the hunt differently. You won't find fancy words or high fallutin' sentence structure that would make any of my English teachers proud. What you will find is real down to earth experiences while hunting.

So how about it hunters? Are you ready to go? Put on your favorite camo hat and kick back in your old tree stand. Maybe fill the Stanley up with coffee and grab a moon pie. Stop after each chapter and think about how your life has been so similar.

Whatever you need to do to get yourself ready, do it! Then come with me on a few hunts and experiences learning Life's Lessons for the Hunter.

Bart McMillan

LIFE'S LESSONS

THE
COMPASS

My Dad at Wham Brake

THE COMPASS

While seated in the bottom of our old John boat, I couldn't help but be transfixed by my father's constant stare at a small round object in his hand. With a flashlight in his mouth and one hand on the motor, my father seemed to guide the boat by this object in his hand. Watching Dad act this way, like I'd never seen him do before, was only the first of many firsts I would experience on this cold November morning.

My dad had been a duck hunter for as long as I could remember. I grew up watching and experiencing the rituals and fevers this epidemic adventure had inflicted on my family. Even at my young age, I had already heard of the assaults my dad and his brothers had made on the black jacks (ring neck scalps), woodies (wood ducks), and the king of ducks, the maw maws (mallards). I remember days and nights spent untangling the lines and the smell of our old fiber decoys. Moss and duck weed still laced the bottom of old Susie and a few decoys that were unnamed due to the wear of their colors. Occasionally, when I would ask the question, "Who is John Whitmire or Jeff Smith?" they would all just laugh and tell how the strays found new homes. It wasn't uncommon for decoys to break hold of their masters' ponds and find their way to the banks for recovery and new ownership. A bad day would suddenly become a banner day when two or three orphans were adopted.

As soon as I discovered the possibility of experiencing the journey into the duck hunter fraternity, I began a steady pursuit for permission to join. My mom never had a chance. She bargained, cried, threatened, and gave a wonderful dissertation on the dangers of duck hunting. However, the inevitable had to happen. By golly, my dad had a son, and part of the Louisiana ritual into manhood including duck hunting. Therefore, at five years old my search for manhood began its life long journey into sleepless nights, bone cold mornings, ridiculous financial reasoning, and the art of lying. In the wake of this journey, I've left cluttered carports, old black milk jugs, and the women of my life to worry from 4:15 a.m. until the door opened to a battle weary duck soldier. What I've found on this journey have been lessons for life.

I can still remember the feeling of anticipation I had that November night before opening day. When morning finally came, I awakened in the darkness of the room I shared with my older sister. A few things step out of my hall of memory. First was the way my mom felt it her responsibility to make sure I looked like a camouflage snowman. Layers produced warmth in her mind and I had on several layers. We were poor and never owned Gortex or Thinsulate. The plastic lining in my boots was Wholesome Bread sacks Mom put over my socks to keep them dry just in case a five year old boy had to stomp a puddle or two. I wore two pairs of brown socks Dad had already worn sometime that week and my gloves were the same as my socks. My knit sweater cap had the smell of saliva I had put there while chewing on it outside in the cold and my jacket was Dallas Cowboy blue. Dad's layers were topped off with the big fur lined coat my uncle brought him back from the Vietnam War. Dad regularly boasted of its warmth and said how he wished everyone could afford such a nice coat.

We got in my dad's old Hoopy ('63 Chevrolet Impala), yes the one with the seats that left bubble marks on your legs in the Summer. We picked up my uncles at their houses where we loaded the motor in the trunk and the boat on the top with wood planks to hold the old John. I sat in the middle of the front seat with my chin on the dash (in the days before seatbelts) and listened as these well-seasoned duck warriors described how the sky would get black as night and foes would fall all around as they carried out their battle plans. My eyes and ears were a database for the second language I learned in the classroom of Hoopy.

We finally arrived at Wham Brake. Wham was a large reservoir that International Paper Company had built to hold their run off from the chemical cleaning of the logs they turned into paper. The water was as black as coffee. I used to enjoy watching the old 6hp Johnson turn up the water and duck weed into a recipe for fine five star duck dining. The smell of Wham was something that tattooed itself into my smelling memory forever. It's the kind of smell you continually complain about, but long to experience again.

After everything was secured in the boat, my turn came to take my place in the back of the John between my father's legs. It's amazing how this location seemed to be a haven of protection and warmth amidst the treacherous dangers my mom had preached about so often. On this particular morning, fog blanketed the brake. My uncles were in session with my father devising a plan to conquer this obstacle. Here's where the life's lesson begins.

My two uncles used an old carbine light hooked up loosely to an old car battery. My dad held something round in his right hand that guided us. Dad never looked up. His eyes were fixed on that round object and his breath gave morse code to the numbers he would count. Finally we stopped. Dad shut off the motor and pierced the silence with proud navigator cheers celebrating the successful crossing of the Delaware (Wham in this case). We had arrived at the duck blind. I don't remember much about the rest of the day. I do remember climbing on top of the blind, watching and listening as the band played their songs of victory over the deceived foe.

The Bible says, "The word is a lamp for the feet and a

light to the path," Psalms 119:105. The one true lesson of life I will never forget is the necessity of a compass. For man, the Bible is that Compass. I would use this lesson many times over as the adventures of hunting took me into the depths of darkness. I would also instill this lesson into the hearts of my own boys.

Somehow today so many young men get lost in the fog of life. Darkness curtains young men into a brake of lostness. Not only did my father guide me with a compass in his hand, but he also placed a compass in my heart. Through the many hours we spent planning and preparing for the adventure of duck hunting, I learned about life. I learned about life's choices, how to be a man, how to survive and pursue dreams and yes, how to know which path to take. Duck hunting is more than a journey into the field, woods, or marsh. Duck hunting is about relationships, investments, and imparting heritage. We still today drag out the old stories and share how our conquest through duck hunting has taken us through life, death, and tough times.

Ironically, six years ago the tables turned. My father went with me to my favorite spot in Texas. Fog again veiled the path. Then, as time stood still, the student led the master with one hand on the motor and one hand holding the compass. We arrived at the same place we had journeyed toward thirty years earlier. And we arrived together.

THE COMPASS

GET IN
THE BOAT

My two sons wearing their face masks to help them keep warm

GET IN THE BOAT

I loved to go hunting in the bean field of Darbone Bayou. Two years earlier a farmer had lost the fight to save his land from the beavers and falling soybean prices. He let his land go to nature and nature took the reins. This land would later become one of the largest wildlife management areas in Louisiana, but we were there first. The flooded pockets of water from the bayou and dammed creeks made a haven for ducks. Here was the first place I saw the sky painted black with ducks. Ducks of every kind found the bean field a sanctuary. We found the same sanctuary a fine place to worship as well.

Hunting in the bean field gave me an outdoor classroom for life's lessons.

I was only thirteen when my dad gave my best friend and me permission to build our own duck blind. Dad suggested I select a location for my blind that was in sight of his. I picked a spot as far away as possible, yet still close enough for dad's approval. But there was one big problem. The spot we had selected for our palace was separated from Dad's blind by the gulf of Darbone Lake. How was I going to cross the head high water between my dad's blind and my own? A boat was the simple solution, but I knew with our five dollar waders and our adventures to the store to sell empty coke bottles, buying a boat was out of the question.

I was taught young that I could do anything if I set my mind to it. So I did. I went to the attic and tore up a sheet of 3/4 inch plywood. I drew a plan out and began to measure and mark on the old 4 x 8 sheet. With my Black and Decker jig saw, I cut out the "Titanic of Duck

Sea." I began to nail my yacht together and before long it looked like a boat.

Dad usually got home about 5:00 p.m. each evening. On the evening I finished my boat, I stood out at the end of the driveway with the incredible anticipation of showing my masterpiece. Dad arrived on schedule and we raced to the carport, his old Chevy Impala against me in my blue Pay Less Tracker tennis shoes. I won by the way. I walked Dad around back of the house to the boat I had built. If there was any doubt, fear, or resentment to my yanking up the plywood, I never detected it. Dad simply said, "Well, let's try it out before we go hunting in it."

The next day was Saturday and a great day to take the maiden voyage. We borrowed my papa's old '69 Ford F100 truck and off we went to the nearest river ramp. Here, my dad gave me one of the bravest and best lessons I have ever experienced. He got in the boat with me! You can't imagine how much water was coming in.

Dad had found an old Folgers coffee can in the truck and brought it along. He was bailing and I was paddling. Dad never said, "Stop. It won't work." He just continued to bail and let me paddle. I also learned something else as I paddled around in circles. Without guides on the bottom of the boat, it won't paddle straight.

Finally, we made it back to the bank with wet feet and knees and my very defeated spirit. Dad helped me get the water logged boat back in the truck. I was quiet. Out of the silence, Dad began to ask questions, "Do you think we might be able to seal the leaks with some wax or tar?" and "Maybe we could put a guide on the bottom so it will go straight." I couldn't speak at the time for fear of crying, but he could tell that his wisdom lifted me out of my embarrassing immaturity. Psalms 25:4-5 "Show me your ways, O LORD, teach me your paths; guide me in your truth and teach me, for you are God my Savior, and my hope is in you all day long." I believe that God uses dads to be an example of how God shares

His truth and love with us in times of need.

We did fix that boat. And because of it I learned a lot and killed a lot of ducks. Two important lessons that stick out are the need for guides and the need for a dad who will get in the boat. A lot of young men today feel very alone in their adventures in life. They need someone to get in the boat with them and yes, even allow them to fail. They also need to stop paddling in circles by having a guide or two in their lives. My two boys and even my little girl have been getting into a lot of boats in their young lives and I have tried to help bail them out when needed.

After twenty-five years, Dad and I still get in the boat together. We have been guides to one another along the way to learning life's lessons. What do you say dads? Are you ready to get in the boat? Your kids, and all kids need a guide.

SAFETIES DON'T
ALWAYS WORK

SAFETIES DON'T ALWAYS WORK

Check your gun at the door. Make sure it's unloaded. I
mean make sure! Hunting was as much a part of my
family as Christmas. When we got together for family
reunions, the conversation always led back to a trip to
the woods when my uncles or relatives conquered nature
and harvested God's creations in a magnificent way.
From the time I could walk and talk, I understood that
hunting was a way of life for me and my family. Along
with this heritage came the constant drilling and
teaching of gun safety. No loaded guns in the house, car,
boat, or ATVs. Every trip out was a classroom on safety

protocol that would later be passed down to my own children.

One Saturday afternoon I sat in the lobby of a college waiting for my son to receive his hunter safety course certificate. When he came out he began to explain how he didn't learn anything new, and how I had taught him everything about safety. He made a 98. I was very proud of him and somewhat proud of myself for passing on the same lectures my dad had taught me. As we drove home, my mind began to race back to the worst day of my hunting life.

When I was eleven my dad and I were in a field hunting doves. It was one of those afternoons when he took off work early and picked me up for a late afternoon hunt. The field was covered in goat weed. We saw a few doves fly over in a corner, but we were content, at least Dad was, to stay put. I got bored and sat down beside my dad. We talked about the usual stuff. As we talked, I began to click the safety from off to on. I had done this for about thirty minutes straight when suddenly the gun went off.

Time stood still. My heart stood still. My body went numb and fear was the first thing that entered my mind. I literally couldn't see, hear, or think clearly. It felt like a shock from a light socket, except I couldn't move my body. Neither of us said anything. I really wasn't sure what had happened. What I did know was that my Winchester bolt action 20 gauge had fired and my playing with the safety was the reason. From the direction the gun was pointing I knew I didn't hit anyone. But why couldn't I move? Then it hit me. This Winchester 20 gauge bolt action was my grandfather's, the same one that had been in the hunting accident.

One cold November morning my grandfather and his brother-in-law went for a little squirrel hunt. Ironically, they went to the old home place where my grandfather was born in 1907. The brother-in-law wasn't much of a hunter and didn't know a lot about safety. After a few hours in the woods my grandfather began to walk back to find him. His brother-in-law mistook him for a deer and with that old Winchester shot and killed him. I've wondered if just taking the gun off safety made it discharge. Maybe he was going to make sure of the target before he pulled the trigger. But instinctively he pointed the gun, took it off safety and the gun fired. Two men really died that day. The brother-in-law, due to his guilt, never really lived again.

I knew a little of that feeling as I sat there beside my dad. He was okay. I was okay. But we both were wounded emotionally. He was wounded because he felt he had failed to teach me everything about gun safety. I was wounded because I had let the teacher down. His reaction was the most harsh thing he could have done. He just sat there. He didn't say a word. Maybe his mind had raced back to his dad and how a stupid little mistake can pierce time and change life forever. I don't know what he was feeling, but I was dying inside. After a while, he gently asked me the question, "What if I had been in front of the gun?" I said nothing. In a few minutes we both got up. I unloaded the empty cartridge and walked out with tears coating my eyes. We went hunting again, but never spoke of that time.

A man named David made some terrible mistakes. He even had a man killed. He prayed this prayer to God, "The troubles of my heart have multiplied; free me from my anguish. Look upon my affliction and my distress and take away all my sins." Psalm 25: 17-18. David took the safeties off in his life and found great pain. Yet he also found forgiveness.

Here's what I learned. Safeties don't always work. No matter how sure we are about life and its adventure, there are always accidents. Perhaps that's how we learn the most. I've never made that same mistake again, but I have made others. By the way, my dad picked me up the next day and took me hunting. I didn't want to go, but he knew I needed to. Maybe you have made a mistake. Maybe you thought the safety was on. Hey, learn from your mistake and move on. Most people will forgive you if you let them. I'm sure there are lessons from your life that you could pass on to someone else about safety, letting go, and yes, even forgiveness.

SAFETIES DON'T ALWAYS WORK

BIGGER DOESN'T
MEAN BETTER

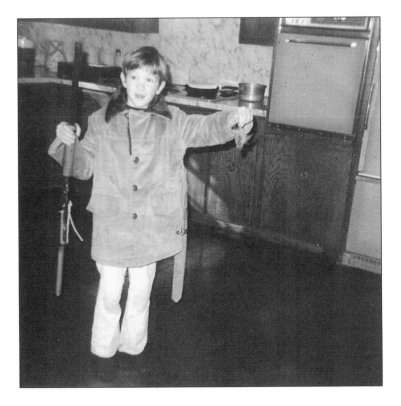

Me and my Red Ryder take our first bird

BIGGER DOESN'T MEAN BETTER

When did you break into manhood? When was the first time that you felt, deep down inside, "Hey, I'm on my way to being a man?" Now, you ladies please forgive me, I don't even know how to ask you the right question. But guys, it was that time when you knew in your heart, "Wow! I have put my feet in the blocks and the gun has fired. I am off and running." For me it was getting my A-5 Browning 12 gauge shotgun. Take a trip with me back to that time.

From the first time I entered the woods with my dad and

uncles, something set the McMillan brothers apart. It was their guns. They were all the same, the Browning A-5. URRRGGG!! I can remember as a little boy how I looked at an A-5. I can still smell the gun oil and old powder smell that I love to this day. The feel! Man, you can't believe how that light 12 felt to a young boy. The feel was power. The feel of that gun went deep into my heart. It felt like home, a place I wanted to be, a position I wanted to be in. I could hear the gun. Not the boom of an old Winchester shell firing. No, the whisper. The sound of the breach that promised, "One day. One day, you'll be a part of the club." And the look. No other gun had that look. Except the Remington Copy Cat or some other wannabe. No the A-5 was distinct. The classy old beaver tail stock and slender forearm were rich with tradition. I get chills thinking about it now. Yes this gun was the biggest, and best.

The day for me was my fifteenth birthday. That would be my starting line for manhood and I will never forget it. I went with my mom to the biggest hunting store in town. They had at least ten A-5s on display. Each was a little different. Each had a little different color to its stock. The ribbed barrels had just come out, and wow! I knew I couldn't miss with that new addition. I went home with a local hunting magazine and ordered all of the free gun magazines in the back. The magazines rolled in. I memorized every make and model of the barrel, size, length, choke, and stock. You name it, I knew it about the A-5. Mom and I must have visited that store at least ten times. Every time, I had to hold them all. I even smelled them. You know what I mean. It's like that old leather baseball glove. Nothing smells quite like it.

The day finally came and we went to the store. It was one of those days you dreamed about, that took forever to arrive. You see, getting this gun meant I was equal. It meant I stood in line with the family tradition. I was the next generation of McMillan men that would step into the woods alone, independent, approved. I was A

MAN, or at least that's what I thought. When we picked it out, I chose a light walnut stock with a ventilated 28" modified barrel. Holy Moly! It was good. No. It was great! I took it home in the box, read every detail in its manual and then assembled it and released the breach at least fifty times to hear that ring sound. My A-5 was all I had hoped for. All I had dreamed, well . . . not yet entirely.

The next day was to be our maiden voyage together. Dad suggested I use some light six shot just to get used to the kick. Hey, not me! I went out and bought copper coated two shot magnums. I can still see those twenty five beasts lined up ready to devour the enemy. We got up early the next morning and headed to the blind. We had perfect duck weather. The temperature was twenty-five degrees and it was sleeting with a wind chill of about five degrees. As we drove to the blind in the boat, ice froze on the barrel.

While it was still dark we could hear the ducks whistling

overhead but we couldn't see them yet. Dad built a fire
in an old metal Coleman ice chest we had dragged up
from the shore and we hovered around it for warmth.
Then the time came. Daylight broke. I loaded my A-5
with the beasts, three of them. My dad shook his head
and began to call. Then, "Here they come. Get down."
Heart pounding, I looked through the willow branches.
There they were, ten to fifteen black jacks. "Take 'em!"

The next few moments passed in slow motion for me. I
placed the gun to my shoulder, took careful aim, and
pulled the trigger. Then the pain began. The magnum
beast embedded its kick into my shoulder. It was so
painful that I pushed the gun away as quickly as possible.
The only problem with that was, I still had my finger on
the trigger. As the gun reached the maximum arm
length from my shoulder, my finger pulled the trigger
again. This time the butt of the gun wasn't on my
shoulder. It was in front of my face. The force of the
gun squared up on my nose. Do you know how many
grams of powder are in a magnum load? Too many for

your nose to take! At this point I went backwards. Dad caught the gun as I landed on the floor with a fountain of blood spouting from my nose. Well, there I was. Did I mention how cold it was? Do you know how sensitive your nose is in the cold? Hmmm.

Looking up through the blood on my face, I watched as Dad unloaded the gun and propped it in a corner. Then he dispelled the one fear that had occurred to me on the way to the store. Would I still be taken care of? One thing is for sure. I did take my first steps toward manhood, but I didn't make it all of the way. No. It was just a step, a step to be followed by many more. I had a lot more ahead of me, and I still do. Do you?

When did you take your first step? Do you remember? Some men are spoiled boys. They never took that step. Maybe no one ever gave them that right of passage. Maybe someone did but wasn't there to keep them walking. Paul says in 1 Corinthians 13:11, "When I was a child, I talked like a child, I thought like a child, I reasoned like a child. When I became a man, I put childish ways behind me." Have you put away childish things? Instead of going for the magnum, bigger and/or better, do you go for the best, most appropriate? No offense guys, but a 3 1/2 magnum? What's up with that?

In the days of knights, there were stages to earn knighthood. You first became a page, then a squire, and only after these steps were completed could you become a knight. I wanted to skip the steps and go to the magnum. Do you?

I still carry my A-5. It's twenty-three years old and still going strong. It's also a reminder of who I am and who I was. If you don't have a mark of manhood in your family, come up with one. Give your children something that separates them from their childhood. Help them make that first step and then walk with them. Later, they will walk on their own.

I just gave my oldest son his Browning. It's a good thing. We are taking steps together now. Let the young hunters learn from life's lessons, but be there to catch the gun when they fall, prop it in a corner and still take care of them.

BIGGER DOESN'T MEAN BETTER

A TRAIN, A RACE,
A DEATH

Great days at the lodge, with great friends

A TRAIN, A RACE, A DEATH

I was a hundred and fifty yards from land on a railroad bridge with a train coming. Have you ever done any illegal hunting and thought you could get away with it? Well I did, but I did not get away with it.

There is nothing like hunting with your best friends. Billy Joe, Kerry and I could read each other's minds. You know how it is. Something will happen. Someone will do or say something and you'll all just look at each other and laugh. Billy Joe, Kerry and I knew each other front wards and backwards. With them, I could do what I liked most in the world, hunting, and do it with someone who liked it as much as I did. For me, spending time with them was like having the best of both worlds.

Billy Joe, Kerry and I had done just about everything in life together. Unfortunately not all of it was good. Three teenage boys out on the town or out in the woods could and did get into a lot of trouble. Our problem was we never got caught! We were untouchable, unbreakable, unchallenged, and relentless in our pursuit of the wild. The S.S. Teenager had taken us through calm waters and stormy seas. With each successful voyage the arrogance of our belief in our indestructible godhood grew. We simply thought we were the best at everything, especially being best friends. There's a kind of brotherly love that only true men in battle can ever experience. When you place your life in the hands of someone who knows you and he still brings you back alive, that's true friendship.

Billy Joe, Kerry and I had headed out for an opening day assault on the duck population. We were going to the first blind I had ever built, my own blind, at my own selected lake. It was my choice, when, where, how, and why. We had selected a place out at Wham Brake, a great place for duck hunting. On a bad day we saw five hundred.

Our transportation was provided by an old wood Skeeter with a 6hp Johnson Dad had passed down to me and my friends. The blind was unbelievable. We built a 16' x 8' blind with a shooting porch, stove, bathroom, carpet, and grill. Our plans included spending the night inside of the blind and opening the season the next morning from within this Taj Mahal on the water.

We woke up early opening day, cooked a few honey buns in butter and then sat on top of the blind to smoke a few Swisher Sweets and listen to the whistle of ducks flying over. What could be better than being in the blind with your best friends, ducks everywhere and a Swisher Sweet hanging out of your mouth. We were in heaven. The day went great! We got our limits and then the trouble began. It was time to stop hunting right? Somehow when you're fifteen, conservation tends to be overruled by greed. Kerry had to go home so we sent the limit with him, but Billy Joe and I planned to stay out and hunt the evening to get one more limit. The only problem with this plan was our being checked at the dock. We couldn't bring any more out. But that didn't stop us. We justified our actions in our minds by saying there would be days we didn't get our limit and today would make up for it.

We had a great hunt that evening. Have you ever shot Black Jacks? Man! They come in groups like teal. We could kill ten each due to the 100 point system. You remember those days don't you? However, we still had the problem. How would we get the ducks out? What if the same game boys were there? We had to have a plan.

There was a train bridge crossing the brake just before you got to the dock. If we waited until pitch dark we could throw the strap of ten ducks over the top and retrieve them later by running down the bridge and picking them up. Great plan, right? Everything went according to plan at first. We went under the bridge. Billy Joe threw the strap on top. The bridge was barely head high from the water so don't give him too much credit. Then we went to the boat dock. Sure enough the same game boys were there. They searched everything. They knew something was wrong but found no evidence.

Smugly, we walked around, loaded up the trailer, and headed off. About a quarter of a mile down the road the train tracks crossed the highway. The plan was for me to get out, run and retrieve the ducks, and Billy Joe would turn around and come pick me up. Well, I got out of the truck and began to run down the bridge toward the ducks. Billy Joe left to turn around. All was smooth until I reached the ducks in the center of the brake about a quarter of a mile from land in either direction. Did I mention we were having alligator problems on that end of the brake?

The plan began to unravel when Billy Joe returned. The Game Warden met him at the bridge. I lay down on the tracks so as not to be seen. It seemed like an hour had passed when a vibration beneath my chest caught my attention. As I looked up the tracks, I could see a train coming at fifty miles an hour. It was time to pray and I prayed better when I was running. I began to run down the track as fast as I could toward the truck. The train's vibrations shot up my spine as my feet hit the ties. Billy Joe was at the bridge by now, but he was on the wrong side of the track to help me escape. I could hear the familiar bells of the crossing signal as the long gates lowered. I tripped and fell hard. There was water on both sides and, I just knew, gators waiting for a skinny fifteen year old to fall in. I began to make deals and bargains with God. I don't know how but it was then that I discovered I needed help. I wasn't indestructible and twenty ducks of any kind were not worth my life. I ran and jumped off the side at the last possible moment where pain, gates, cars and land would intersect. I don't know if it was divine intervention or what, but I made a hard, sure landing on land.

Billy Joe came back through and picked me up. We had made it, but we were different. It was quiet for a while. No R.E.O. Speed Wagon pierced our eardrums as usual when we were in his truck. We didn't high five or dip Copenhagen to celebrate. No the cab was loud with silence and fear.

Have you ever wanted to throw up or go gag yourself to get that sick feeling out of your stomach? Our theology changed also. That night was a wake up call. Neither one of us had respected nature or life that day, but God had played a role in our hunt. He had saved us both from jail and me from death. This event set in motion a search. Was God real? Did he care? Up to that point I had just assumed because of the wild life I lived, I was going to Hell so I didn't care about trying to be good. But not long after that night, I sat in the back of a small church and heard about a man who died for me so that I wouldn't have to die. I heard about how He took all of the wrongs I had done and gave me the chance to be forgiven, to start all over again. Wow! That was what I needed. I remember going to the front of that church that night, getting on my knees and praying a prayer that went like this, "Dear God, I am sorry I have done a lot of things wrong in this world. I have lived fifteen years of my life for me. I want to live the rest of my life for you. The Bible says, "For God so loved the world that he gave his one and only Son, that whoever believes in him shall not perish but have eternal life." John 3:16

Guys, I can't begin to explain to you the love and forgiveness I felt. I truly stood up a new person. I changed. Everything I had ever done wrong didn't matter. I was forgiven. More importantly I met the God who saved me that night spiritually, but who had saved me physically several times when I wasn't even aware of it. Listen hunters. I'm going to ask you a gut question. It's just you and me. Do you know Jesus as your Savior? Has He saved you spiritually? I'm sure He has protected you physically, but has He saved you spiritually? It's time to start over. It's time to trade gods. How about making Jesus the God of your life. Your friends will be glad you did. My friends were, and soon afterwards they did too. Your family needs you to. Your God wants you to. Well, how about it? How about right now getting down on your knees and talking to God? He loves you and has a lot of great things in store for you.

I've had some great hunts since that time. They were great in a different way from that point on. I learned that hunting had nothing to do with killing, but everything to do with who you're with, where you're at in life and who you really are. You will too if you take that step and pray. Is it time for you to pray?

THE
AB CLIMBER

Guaranteed to help you lose weight

THE AB CLIMBER

Ever been in a tree climbing deer stand? Ever been in a tree climbing deer stand that wouldn't go down? Let me just tell you how this story unraveled from the beginning.

My pastor gave me a tree stand. Wow! I was pumped. You know it's not that I really needed a tree stand. I just wanted one. I don't know what it is about us men, but we want every new gadget that comes out. Remember the electric toe socks? Got 'em. How about the laundry detergent for our camo that would make sure the deer couldn't see or smell us? I got that too. By the way, my wife put my freshly washed invisible to deer camos in the dryer with a Snuggle fabric softener sheet. You would have thought I was wearing a Glade plugin around my neck when I entered the woods.

Back to the stand. I had been envious, no jealous, no I had been downright covetous of those guys every Saturday morning that would climb high into the tree, lie back, and make life seem so good. ESPN makes it look easy don't they? Even the dang camera man is highly set in his lounge chair in the sky.

I had gone out in the back yard several times and lassoed a tall pine with my climber. It wasn't all that hard, but I knew at 5:00 a.m. with binoculars, rattles, scents, range finder, wind strips and bow, getting up the tree would be a difficult task. As a matter of fact, I was reluctant to even try it on the few mornings I had to get into the woods. But not my son. Oh NO! Micah wanted to use the climber. He had drooled over it from the first day he saw it. I tried to talk him out of it, but he was determined to scale a tree, draw a bow, and harvest the trophy buck of his life. He was like the rest of us men. Greed and adventure overtook him.

Bow season was right around the corner and Micah had been practicing for weeks. He had killed a deer earlier with a gun and was now ready to move to the bow. I had spent two years teaching him the difference between killing and hunting, the difference between killing and harvesting. For the most part he learned well. Because he grasped that hunting was the true adventure, it naturally meant that harvesting a deer with a bow would be a real challenge for a true hunter.

You know it takes a lot of preparation to get a buck, so we went out to a small private strip of woods to check for signs. Sure enough, there were signs everywhere. We saw scrapes and pawed out ravines for the young lady deer to notice. We put out salt blocks and that stuff you pour into the ground. Listen, if Wal-Mart carried it and it attracted deer, we put it out.

On the way back from the woods, I talked to Micah about the importance of practicing with the climber in the back yard. I told him the importance of going up and down a tree several times, and even shooting from the stand twenty feet off the ground. After my speech about practice, I was rewarded with a teenage sigh and a few knowing comments from the next Bill Dance of deer hunting so I shut up. He did go shoot out of the stand for about ten minutes, with it two feet off the ground. Hey, he's fourteen. I should have just saved my breath.

Morning came. Bow season was here and my boy was ready. In his mind he was totally prepared to go. I didn't have a bow so I planned to just stay in the car until he called on the walkie talkies we shared. We got up early, loaded everything up, stopped by the local store for our usual powdered donuts and coffee, (Dr. Pepper for the teenager), and headed out to the woods. We unloaded everything from the SUV and headed to the tree we had chosen beforehand for Micah to make his maiden voyage to bow hunting paradise. The adventure begins here. Did I mention he was fourteen? A teenager?

Everything was in place around the tree for him to start his journey up. I stood below to give guidance and encouragement. The first five feet were okay. Then, a few comments about how he couldn't see and how it felt like he was high enough started coming out. He was eyeball level to me. "That couldn't be high enough," I said. In the Georgia mountains it's always cool in the morning. This particular morning was downright cold and Micah had his coveralls on. You get the picture. He was hot, tired and bulky. Nevertheless, on he went until about fifteen feet up which he declared the stopping point. I agreed and he settled in. Of course if you've ever been on a climbing stand you know what that seat's like. And how about that feeling that you're going to drop something or even fall out? I knew all of this was going to hit him like a ton of bricks, but you know what, he had to learn for himself.

I went back to the SUV and did a little catch up work from the office. It was kinda cool. The sun came up and showed off its colors and power over the earth. It's easy to understand how people worship nature. A couple of hours passed by and the walkie talkie began to click and clatter. I felt like this might be the great hunter's way of saying, "I can't take it anymore." Sure enough, I arrived at the deer stand and there he was, mad, hot, and sore. He started describing the engineering flaws that in his estimation the climber had. Then he began to talk about the dogs. "What dogs?" I said. Apparently, the attractants we had put out also attracted the local dogs. Everything in me wanted to laugh, but I could tell he was in no mood for me to make the situation any more difficult. He lowered his bow and other supplies. Then he began the challenge to come down from the tree.

You would think coming down would be easier than going up. Not for him. We, and I do mean we, began a match between the tree, the climber, my suggestions, and Micah's fatigue. It was brutal. It was also hilarious. For twenty minutes he tried turning every way in the world. He lifted his feet, pushed on his toes while lifting with his heels, or was it lifting the bottom platform with his heels and lowering with his toes. One thing for sure, he wasn't making any progress. As a matter of fact, he was going up, not down! Panic set in. "I'll just jump," he said. "No," I replied, "You'll break something." We went over and over how he was to lower the bottom and put his weight on the rails of the upper stand. That didn't work. Nothing worked. Somehow during this struggle we began to laugh and I mean just roll. He started a commentary from his now permanent home up the tree describing how he was going to sue the company, picket the local sporting goods store and save other hunters from this torture. Then he came up with a great plan.

Have you ever seen that ab machine on TV? It's guaranteed to help you lose hundreds of pounds and give you that washboard stomach? Well, Micah began a

commercial like this, "It's the Ab Climber! You may
have seen other ab machines on TV, but NO machine
works like this one. I guarantee, you will lose all of the
weight you want. Yes, if you go up, you won't come
down. And how about those abs? After a few hundred
attempts trying to get down, your gut will be lean and
mean. Yes, you thought the Ab Climber was just for
hunters. No! Give it to anyone. Especially the people
you want to get away from. You may never see them
again. And if you do they will thank you for the free
vacation they received. Yes, you can have the Ab
Climber for half the original price if you call right now.
But wait! That's not all! If you call right now, you will
receive absolutely free a roll of toilet paper and an
umbrella, because you ain't going anywhere anytime
soon."

We just howled! You know James 1:2-4 says, "Consider
it pure joy, my brothers, whenever you face trials of
many kinds, because you know that the testing of your
faith develops perseverance. Perseverance must finish its

work so that you may be mature and complete, not lacking anything." Micah was surely being tested. After forty-five minutes he finally jumped to a nearby tree limb and worked his way down the branches. He learned a lot that day, like the importance of practice. He learned that before you embark on a new adventure you'd better be ready. Now he understands that old saying, pay now or pay later.

How about it hunters? Have you ever gotten yourself into a position that you weren't prepared for? Maybe you just didn't know it was going to cost you so much. Going into it, everything seemed easy, but once you were there you seemed trapped. You panicked. You jumped trees. I've seen a lot of dads do that with their families. It's no laughing matter when it comes to little girls and boys are left stranded. I'm not going to be very nice here. Men, it's time to grow up. For some reason men have a hard time putting others first, especially their families. And boy are we paying a high price in our country. Boys and girls today need dads more than ever.

I've worked with thousands of teens for nineteen years. Nothing influences their lives like a true dad. In the book *Raising Boys*, James Dobson show an alarming reality that when dads aren't around, kids' grades fall, and the number of kids involved in drug use, teen pregnancy, and suicide goes up. Get the picture! I told a dad just recently when he asked the question, "Should I stay married just for my children?" Yes! Yes! Yes! How about putting someone else before yourself? Can you think of a better reason to stay married in the whole world? Some guys need to get together and take him behind the woodshed if you know what I mean. Life will not always be easy. Life will not always put you in a situation you are prepared for. That's when you truly mature and grow. Micah paid the price that day with the climber because he wasn't prepared. He also took the chance of losing his tree stand and supplies.

We rescued the Ab Climber and I keep it in the garage. I like having it around as a reminder to us that we must practice and we must count it pure joy when tough

times hit. That's when we will truly grow in character. You may be in a tough tree right now. Don't jump! Let God use this time to develop some real character in you. In the meanwhile, keep practicing. The real challenges are ahead.

IT'S NOT
HIS NATURE

My princess

Trouble is,
trouble does,
pure "d" trouble

Micah on opening dove day

A pose for the girls

IT'S NOT HIS NATURE

I was twelve years old, lying on top of the monkey bars with my best friend at the elementary school playground down the street. It was 10:00pm and he asked the question, "When you have kids, whatcha gonna have?" Of course we assumed at that time I had a choice. I looked up at the stars and said, "Two boys and a girl." "Why a girl?" he asked. I replied, "Well, I need two boys, one to fish and one to hunt and I need a girl to cook what we bring home." I got my wish. I have my two boys and beautiful girl. I have also learned some lessons about the challenges of raising three very different individuals.

Somewhere along the journey of life, when we truly mature, we realize that we are not on the earth to mold children, but to guide them. I've also learned that my plans aren't easily accepted by my own children. God made them unique, different, and dad-gum-it sometimes I can't figure out whose loins my kids are from. When they succeed, I take full credit. However, when those three rascals of mine get into trouble, I humbly remind my wife that they take after her side of the family.

Micah's the oldest. He's in high school. So far he would rather spend his birthday with Dad camping out or going to find a Spring turkey. Micah's my hunter. He loves it. He eats, drinks, and sleeps hunting. We've spent a lot of days together in the field, but no matter how many times we go, he can't get enough! Every day has its adventures, its lessons and its epilogue. Many nights we've curled up together, falling asleep to some of the old hunting stories passed down from one generation to the next.

Maybe it's the teacher in me but I see every trip as an opportunity to learn and grow as friends with my son. Now don't get me wrong. I am not his buddy. I am his adult friend. But more importantly, I am his dad. Not his father, his dad. Fathering a child is something any male can do. My goal is being a dad.

Matthew, my second son, is a fisherman. I've tried on several occasions to teach Matthew the art of hunting. He's just not there. His mother and I say, "It's not his nature," and you know what? It's not. But he loves the feel of the rod and reel in his hands. And I love spending time with my son doing what he loves to do.

Now my little girl doesn't do much cooking but she and I do go hunting together. We go hunting in the mall. Macie is a good hunter. She'll wound a few clothes racks and call in a few deals. But more importantly, we bag our limit together and she has fun with her dad.

I've been around a lot of dads who spend a tremendous

amount of time trying to make certain things out of their children. The fact is all kids are different. Micah likes to hunt and Matthew likes to fish. It's not the same joy when they are doing something they aren't cut out to do. It's just not their nature.

I heard a wise man speak about a favorite scripture passage, "Train up a child in the way he should go and when he is old he will not depart from it." Proverbs 22:6 KJV. At face value this verse seems to say teach a child what he ought to do and when he is old he will do it. Wrong! That's not what it really says. A better understanding of the verse is, "Train up a child in the area he is bent toward and even when he is old he will still go in that direction." I see many parents trying to force their children into being something that's just not in them to be. It's not their nature. The result is *rebellion*.

I sure do like hunting with my little hunter, fishing with my little fisherman, and doing girl stuff like shopping with my little girl. I am truly blessed with three different, distinct, and driven children. All in all hunting has never been sweeter than the times I do it with them. When I take to the fields of life with these three, it's not about me. It's about them, their nature, their success.

Children learn more, with more enthusiasm, and listen better to the sermons that we parents preach when they're placed in their own favorite arena of life. So dads, stop trying to make your children fit a mold you have dreamed up for them. What is your child bent toward? Train him in that area, even if it's not hunting. (Did I say that?) Find out your child's natural bent. Hey, if you don't have a child of your own, find a kid without a dad. You'll enjoy the hunt with a kid along and who knows, you may help them discover their true nature.

ONE COLD
TURKEY

Micah's first turkey

ONE COLD TURKEY

For three years my son and I had been in pursuit of the big tom. We got turned on to turkey hunting when we moved to Georgia. After a few deer, duck and dove trips in the East, it was time to take on the Spring challenge of the bearded gobbler. Now let me tell you, I'm not a traditionalist when it comes to turkey hunting. Some men want to make the hunt a moment to be recorded on a Hallmark card. Not me and my son. As soon as we get close enough, be warned. We are going to kill the first tom or jake that walks by.

We traveled to the closest Wal-Mart and bought a variety of box calls plus several mouth calls that were on clearance. A little while later I wanted to slap the guy who invented mouth calls. Those lip tickling things drove us crazy! Calling turkeys is downright hard. Finally, I found the slate call. We soon had turkeys gobbling all around. We had turkeys flying over, turkeys running away, and turkeys staying just out of range to harvest. Until finally, one April day we found success.

Early that morning my son woke me up saying, "Let's go get a tom." With three years of unsuccessful trips pulling hard on my eyelids, I groaned to myself, "Oh man!" But he was persistent. He loaded the truck, even cranked it up. I finally gave in, crawled out of bed, threw on some Mossy Oak and we headed out. We set up just as we had dozens of times before. When I came fully awake, I realized I was glad to be out in the woods with my boy. That was enough for me.

All of a sudden a big old tom stuck his head over the

ridge and gobbled. Our hearts started to play the male kettle beat passed on by the early settlers. That tom began to strut, but he wouldn't come any closer. So as soon as the tom snuck back over the ridge, I dashed a mad sprint of about thirty yards away from the ridge and where I had been sitting. At this point I couldn't see my son, but he knew what to do. I began a yelp on the slate and in just a matter of seconds the gun went off. I sprinted back toward the ridge and saw my son, the great conqueror of turkey land, raise his harvest toward the clouds. We had a man moment, one where you just want to spit together and declare those woods holy ground. No man before or after would ever spill the blood of a turkey in a better way than me and my son. Wow! It was great!

After taking a lot of pictures and showing everyone in town, I called several taxidermists to ask about having the tom mounted. By the time I had searched out the best deal, the old tom had been sitting in the freezer for nine months. We finally agreed the best thing to do was to cut off the beard and tail and eat the sucker. We laid that turkey out on the kitchen table to thaw. My wife wasn't too happy about the new resting place, but I informed her it wouldn't be long til I would move it, just until it thawed out. Have you ever looked at a turkey's head? Ug-ly! That was probably the second ugliest head I had ever seen.

One day passed and the turkey was still as hard as a rock. We left the turkey on the table, over my wife's protests, for another day. My son and I would walk by and rehash the battle story embellishing it with a few manly grunts. It was really cool to us, but my wife wasn't very happy about the whole thing. I decided hey, she'll get over it. I checked the turkey on the third day and it was still as hard as a rock. How could that be? That turkey had been sitting out for three days! Through nine meals we had looked at that ugly head. Then it hit me, the feathers. Feathers are the best insulation in the world. I plucked that bird and in a matter of a few short hours, it thawed out. We moved it from the table, much to my wife's relief, cooked it and it was good. However, my son and I were the only ones who ate any.

Here's the lesson for life. Sometimes we put insulation on ourselves. Sometimes we insulate our lives and even our hearts to the point where we stay hard and unaffected by the love of people around us. We insulate our hearts with bad attitudes, hurt feelings, broken relationships, and disappointment. We also insulate ourselves with good things like success, money, hobbies and work. Eventually we become numb to the really important things and important people around us.

In Acts 28:27 the Bible says, "For this people's heart has become hard, they hardly hear with their ears, and they have closed their eyes. Otherwise they might see with their eyes, hear with their ears, and understand with their hearts." And also in I Samuel 16:7, "Man looks at the outward appearance, but the Lord looks at the heart."

You may have a few broken relationships that need a warm word of hope. Open your life up again. Make your heart open to new experiences and even a few painful things as well. The main thing is for you to open up your heart. I've hunted with some men who were very successful on the outside, but you could tell their heart was cold, frozen solid. It's time to chill out, or in this case, thaw out. Take off the insulation and let your heart get warm.

ONE COLD TURKEY

A TIME TO SAY GOODBYE

Liberty two weeks before her first hunt

Liberty stands over the fallen foe

A TIME TO SAY GOODBYE

Nothing changed my world of hunting like adding a dog to the quest. I've had the privilege of hunting ducks and geese from South Texas to Canada. Wow! I love duck hunting. You know for a while it was the most important thing in the world to me. Then that five foot four brunette walked into my life. I know what you're thinking, "Not another chick flick." Heck no! Not from me dude!. Let's get back to the story. I love duck hunting and it has taken me from plains to marsh, from swamp to fields. I have hunted with some great men and some great dogs, but no dog has ever matched

Liberty. Liberty was my dog, but she was more than just a dog. She was my hunting partner.

I got Liberty the same weekend that the Statue of Liberty was being reopened after renovation in 1986. My wife came up with the name and it sure matched this beautiful black lab that would truly bring freedom to my hunt. With the old Water Dog book a friend had given me, I started a twice daily training regimen. I couldn't believe how fast Liberty learned the art of staying, sitting, and fetching. A wise old hunter saw Liberty in the back window of my car and told me, "Son, if you got a good hunting dog, you won't teach her anything. But if you got a bad hunting dog, you can't teach her anything." Wow. How true that was for Liberty. She grew stronger and faster and became the best duck retriever I had ever seen.

She was only three months old when I took her on her first hunt. I never will forget that day. It was the opening day of teal season in Northeast Texas. We were standing in the riverbed that a dry summer had left behind. Liberty acted perfectly, taking her place beside me in the mud. The sun broke over the old cypress laced fog and the whistle of a group of blue wings jetted overhead. This experience was new for Liberty. She did something then that I would see a thousand times over. Her whole body began to shake. Her eyes strained to see the ducks without moving her head. For the first time in my hunting career, it was more fun to watch something other than the ducks.

Liberty knew. The mood, the smell, the cool breeze, and the crack of gun shots were her heaven. The hunt and this dog were a match. I was just there as her chauffeur. The first flight came in from behind. Two hit the water from my A-5's deadly aim. Liberty acted appropriately. I told her to hold. She did. Then with my heart in my throat I gave the command, "Fetchem up." You would have thought the world stood still. I can still see that little black lab struggling to get a teal back through the mud to my feet. I told her to hold, but she couldn't wait. She turned, sat, and waited for the next command. "Fetchem up!" Off she went. Aiee! I was proud. A game warden came over and laughed at how small she was. Then two teals came by. I shot both. Liberty retrieved as before and he stopped laughing. He offered to buy her on the spot, the first of many such offers in her lifetime. I said no and we went on our way.

Liberty amazed me with some incredible retrieves. She went under water on several occasions, walked on ice, made several double retrieves and found a few birds that I never saw fall. She watched for ducks behind me and I watched in front. I guess there was one time that Liberty's skills really showed her greatness. I had just become friends with a young man who guided in South Texas. Frank had a great dog named BJ. That dog qualified for all types of trials and competitions. I must admit, I was very intimidated by the pedigreed champ. My wife and I had never even taken the time to send off for Liberty's papers.

Liberty and I made a date to go hunting with BJ and
Frank. We got into the ducks big time. Frank would
send BJ out with whistles and commands, precisely given
and precisely carried out. By this time Liberty and I had
gotten so comfortable with our hunting style, she just
knew what to do and when. She didn't miss a beat, or a
duck. I was proud. But the true test would come later
that day.

Frank hit a woody and it glided off. We all got in the
boat and took off after it. When we got to the bank
where the duck had crossed into the woods, Frank sent
BJ. The only problem was, BJ wouldn't go. I couldn't
believe it. BJ was confused. The bank was lined with a
fence of briars. None of us really knew what was on the
other side. To Liberty, it didn't matter. There was a
duck over there somewhere and when she heard,
"Fetchem up," she was off. A few minutes later she
came back with the woody in her mouth. You can't
imagine how proud I was.

We sent both dogs on several more retrieves like this one and Liberty girl trained the champ on how to hunt in the real world. Liberty was recognized by one of the Vice Presidents of a major oil company as the best. She even made the news one dove season as she fetched up a few doves in a local sports show in Houston. In later years she slowed down, but she never stopped. At fourteen, on her last hunt, she retrieved nine Canada geese, four mallards, four grey ducks, two teal and two widgeons. Not one time did I tell her where to sit, stay, fetch or hold. She was one of the hunters.

She was also my wife's and my first baby. We loved her and she was worthy. She had her place in our family on the porch and in the car. If someone tells you, "You can't have a pet and a hunting dog too, " they're wrong. They've just never had a Liberty girl. Everyone loved Liberty.

As the years passed my wife and I had three children. Each child saw Liberty as their nurse when they were sick. She had a good sense of motherhood. No matter how badly the children abused her with bows from dress up or an occasional careless baseball throw, she showed an unusual amount of understanding. Even the grandparents loved Liberty. She had her place in each house when she visited. What a great dog.

We almost lost her a few times, to parvo, pneumonia, snake bites, and once a treble hook. She decided she was a catfish on a fishing trip and swallowed the bait. I would not recommend leaving your rods lying around with cheese bait on the hooks.

On several occasions, Liberty had to watch the house and family when I was out of town. She could do it all. She had her bad days as well. Turning over trash cans and a few chewed up doves caused some anxiety occasionally but all in all, she was the best, a friend, protector, nurse, and hunter.

The last year of her life Liberty had cancer. The bumps

on her side began to bleed. You know, I could have
stood the vet bills and nasty smell, but neither she nor I
could take the way the children pulled back their love.
It wasn't their fault. Cancer can be nasty. I got three
opinions from different vets. They were all the same. It
was time to put her down. I had spent all our years
together keeping her alive. Now I had to take her life. I
can't begin to tell you how difficult that was.

We took her back home to see the grandparents over
Christmas holidays to give everyone a chance to say
goodbye. Then I took her to a field for the last time.
She and I went through some of the old commands.
She was as proud as ever to sit, stay and even fetch up an
old stick. Man I cried. Now guys, I don't mean one of
those whiney cries, I'm talking about a deep cry of pain
from my heart. My soul hurt. I apologized to her and
begged her to forgive me. Her calm brown eyes and
grey beard were the peace I needed to follow through. I
still get tears in my eyes even as I write this. Dad-gum-
it, it hurts to lose a hunting partner, especially one who

always gave and never asked for anything in return.

In Philippians 1:3, Paul says, "I thank my God every time I remember you." Cherish the moments with all of your hunting partners. One day cancer or something else will separate you. I would love to have any hunt, good or bad, to do over again with Liberty, my friends, and my dad. Every trip I take to the field or the stream has a different feel now. I had to say goodbye. We all will you know. Each Winter I still walk out to the woods where we buried her and thank God for the times she protected my family and I didn't know it, for the times she swam over a pot hole that I surely would have drowned in. I miss my hunting partner, but the time came to say goodbye. Remember the important friends in your life. Remember the smell, the sounds and the feel of their presence. It's a little colder in the boat on the way to the blind now. I sure do miss that girl. Remember to thank God for the partners in your life.

My friend Mike

Ben and I get our limit

My 6-wheeler

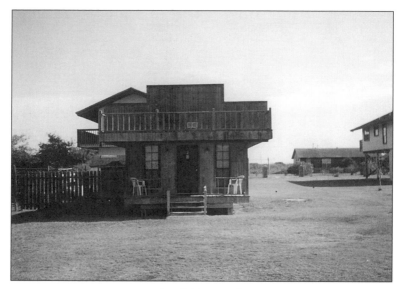

South Texas Lodge

Quail Hunting

Ouachita River

A good day with Kyle, Kevin, Micah

Matthew's first duck

I don't want to brag

Micah's art work

South Texas Lease

Bart McMillan is an Associate Pastor at First Baptist Church, Gainesville, Georgia. He grew up in West Monroe, LA. He has hunted for 33 years from Texas to Georgia, Canada to that Country South of the United States, South Louisiana. Bart has worked with students for 19 years. He is a very gifted speaker that uses humor to share about Life's Lessons and God's love.

Bart is blessed with a beautiful wife and three wonderful children. The most important priorities in his life are his relationship to God, his family, and his world in which God has entrusted him to be a light.

He is working on his next book, "Life's Lessons for The Dad." This book is a light-hearted look at how dads lead their families and how everyone learns about life through their successes and failures.

For more information, you may contact Bart at
Lifeslessons4@aol.com
or write him at
PO Box 67 Gainesville, Ga 30503